Soul & Spirit

by
Tyler Adams

Graphic Design by Breanne Jackson
Edited by Heather Dees
Assisted by April Andrews Denney
Assisted by Shelia Adams

Forwards

The poems in this collection were written by the author, Tyler Adams, as a way to reflect his Christianity and love for Christ. Throughout the collection, Tyler contemplates themes we encounter daily in this life ad how best to celebrate one's personal relationship with Christ in alignment with those themes. Tyler's work is one that is also mirrored in his day-to-day life as a Christian. The words in these poems are both uplifting and guiding, sharing a sense of peace with the reader that is to give over one's life to a power greater than themselves. I have known Tyler for over 30 years. As a lifelong friend, I am thankful for the opportunity to introduce readers to Tyler's inspirational light and joy as both a person and a man of God. While you are reading this collection of poems, I encourage you to pause and reflect on your walk with Christ and the many ways in which He has enriched and blessed your life.

- Quenton Lackey

Tyler Adams is a great guy who faces the challenges of life head-on and full force. Through his life and experiences, he seeks to use his knowledge and talents to help others, whether it is in public speaking, one-on-one conversations, or through his writings. His writing offers him the opportunity to share creativity, and that's a passion he has. Tyler recognizes the power of words to communicate, to heal, and to encourage. He likes to channel the words into a flow that will inspire others. He is a faithful believer in the Almighty God, the One who has guided Tyler through the difficulties of life, and who sustains him. He wants people to know and feel the power of God in their lives, and he evangelizes to help guide others on that path. He wants to draw closer to God and to help others do this, too. So whether you're reading a selection of Tyler's writing that will make you laugh or perhaps bring a tear to your eye, know that you are seeing an insight into a person who loves God, loves people, and wants the best for everyone. So, kudos to Tyler for writing this book!

- Richard Martin

I first met Tyler Adams when he came to Sugar Creek to worship. I served for several years as an elder at Sugar Creek. Tyler took Hebrew 13:17 to heart. From the New King James version it reads, "Obey those who rule over you and be submissive, for they watch out for your souls…" I can't recall one time that Tyler declined to help the congregation when the elders asked. He led singing, prayer, served the Lord's Supper, taught bible class and preached lessons. Tyler is very sincere in his faith in Christ. Tyler gave Dinah and me some of his poems that he wrote. He wrote from the heart. The words are beautiful. He expressed his inner thoughts. He expressed the importance of God being in his life! I have never met someone who could express himself so well in a poem. As you read Tyler's book, you will see what is in Tyler's heart.

- Alton Bailey

Tyler has captured many emotions in his writings and shares them as way of encouraging others through different times of their lives.

- Janice Ritter

In this life journey we are all upon, it is often that we encounter an acquaintance, someone to share a story or simple common interaction. However, it is much more rare that we find someone along our path that is genuine and selfless, who we can consider a true friend. For over two decades, Tyler Adams is one such person that I have had the privilege of knowing and would consider the utmost in devotion to his family, friends, and most importantly to God. He has a deep faith in God that is evident in his life. This faith Tyler possesses is seen as joyous and grateful during times of prosperity but also present and steadfast during trials and storms of life. These characteristics of Tyler are what makes his poetry so endearing. He writes from a deeper perspective of what God promises are to come for His believers. Weather the moment is triumphant or dark that the reader faces, Tyler's poems bring encouragement and comfort to endure and press forward. His writings can help bring peace during conflict and give perspective of the "bigger" picture in life, which is the hope that can only be found in Christ.

- Brandon Cline

Tyler has a unique ability to put everyday thoughts and emotions into words. Regardless of what you have going on in your life now, you will find insight, meaning, and peace reading his work.

- Josh Aaron

I would like to thank Tyler Adams for the opportunity to write a few words about him. Tyler has one of the gentlest spirits of anyone that I have ever witnessed. It seems that everything that he does is done with grace and compassion with a willing heart. I guess you might say, his character is one of true Christianity. His character is seen in everything he does, from preaching the Gospel of Christ to writing poetry that reflects his true belief in Jehovah God. Everyone needs help from the people around them. Tyler is a person willing to help, and I believe the true reason he writes, is to help people realize and know there is a God and that God cares for us. I consider it an hono to know Tyler and consider him a brother, to be involved in his life, t see him overcome adversities, and to see him succeed in so many ways being useful and encouraging in the church and in my life. I wish all the good blessings for him.

- Sincerely Jeff Hancock.

As Christians we begin at the "house of God." We must be aroused t lay hold of our purchased privileges. We mst be challenged once agai to become men and women of prayer, compassion, faith, joy, and holy living. Tyler Adams' work challenges us to reflect and to remember the blessings and what is to come. Masterful!

- Kristopher Johnson

The Lord can use pain and difficult times for the good. It is often through times such as these that causes one to either become bitter ar angry at God or to the contrary and to run toward Him, to seek Him in a deeper and more meaningful way, to grow spiritually and to lov God more. And the latter is exactly what Tyler has done in his life. His spiritual walk has gotten considerably deeper and more meaningful as a result of some of the difficult times that he has endured. In much of Tyler's poetry, he gives the reader insight into mind and soul, and the reader can hear and see the genuineness of th love he has for his Lord. Tyler is a very real, genuine and down-to-earth. He is kind and gentle. He is easy going and patient. He has large capacity to love others and to love his Lord. One can surely say he has a big heart, that he is selfless and giving toward others. He is a very good friend who is reliable and dependable and trustworthy. He doesn't lie and is not pretentious in any way. Yes, Tyler possesses many Christ-like qualities. To know Tyler, one cannot help but to like him. One good way to get to know him is through his poetry. There is value and benefit for the mind, heart and soul to be had from spending some time with his writings. If you are a Christian and you ponder his words and draw upon the spirituality therein, it will help you in your Christian walk. If you are not a Christian, his words will give you some insight about the hope and peace that are afforded by the Christian walk. The reader can see a story being told through his poetry. Some of his poems describe some very difficult and low points in life. Moving forward the story develops more into a life of letting go of hurts, loving and trusting in the Lord and following after Him. Heartache and difficulty are left behind and are replaced by the peace of God. From there develops a happy and fulfilled life. We can all learn a lot by such a journey and be encouraged in our own lives as we go through our own sets of challenges and ups and downs. It is through someone life Tyler and through his poetry that helps us understand more about certain things in life and more about how maybe we should be in certain ways. We genuinely recommend Tyler's writings to you. You will be rewarded by spending time reading his words. You won't regret it.

- Ed and Milla Bluemly

As a young man, the words of the Bible and promises of God often confused me. The words on the page almost speak directly to me, although they were written thousands of years ago and meant for everybody. The promises of God are so deep and engrained in my faith that only a few people can capture and put them into words that adequately describe them. Poets are charged with taking our thought and feelings and making them tangible, as though we can reach out and pluck the out of thin air. Tyler Adams has that natural gift, an his poems are powerful reminders of every promise that God has for us.

- Mitchell Taylor

Everyone will benefit from reading and rereading these beautifully written and artistically illustrated poems about faith and purpose in life. They remind me of King David in Psalms as he recorded his thoughts while experiencing the challenges and rewards of a life centered on God. The resulting words of wisdom are a balm for the soul.

- J. Barry Mason

Poetry has marked the passage of centuries with beautifully worded phrases that captured the hearts of people through the years. It is st studied today and speaks to the souls of so many. Tyler Adams in th book Soul and Spirit shares his thoughts and inspiration from a modern day poet's point of view to encourage and uplift. His poems have been used at weddings and special occasions. This collection is from his heart.

- Phyllis Hoffman DePiano

There are not many people live you that can write poems. There are even fewer people that will write poems about God's word. Therefo it is encouraging to read your poems based on Biblical principles and to understand the thoughts in them.

- Dr. Robert Ham

I am delighted to write this forward, not only because Tyler has been a friend for more than ten years, but also I believe he has a message given from God to inspire, and motivate people of all ages. He is a pillar of the community and has the loving support of his family and friends. Thank you for exemplary character and friendship and your ability to empower others.

- Cedric Allen

Poetry is one of humanity's oldest forms of expression. As literature, poetry is important because the words and phrase are carefully chosen and become memorable to us in the feelings conveyed. This author reveals his heart and his spirituality. Enjoy these poems with me.

- Steve Wilsher

No matter what situation I'm in, I try to see the positive or positive side in life. I always try to see the good in things. Sometimes life wi tear you down, and there seems to be no light at the end of the tunne, but with God's help, you can see light, you will survive, you can mov forward. However, you must do your part and not be complacent. You must keep going, keep moving. Look to God. Find His peace and build on His strength. You have two choices: to own your life or let own you...no regrets! Give all of yourself to God, to family, to friends, and put your heart, your soul, your spirit into your life...

- *T*

Humbly, I Bow

Burdens are Lifted by His Mighty Hand

Held Through Each Journey

Peace

For Me

Blessed Through Faith

Every Day Lord, I Am Thankful

I Will

The Lord is My Strength

Legions of Angels

The River

My Own Faith

Stronger, I Rise

One Day, Lord

Going Home

I'll Be There

When I Get There

That Day I Await

Waiting on Heaven

III.   The Light That Leads Me

Seek First

Be with Me, Lord

Humility

The Walk Each Day

Life's Path

Holding on to Your Hand

Life and Its Storms

Abide with Me, Lord

I'm Praying, Lord

Strength and Faith

Lord, Be with Me

Trials and Temptations

Strength to Choose

Lift Me Up

Trusting the Lord

Strength and Peace

Watch Over Me, Lord

Take Me Home, Lord

IV.   The Heart's Emotions

Only One

A Blessing

You Are the Poem in My Heart

Amazing

Unconditional Love

Only Know to Say

Always and Forever

The Bright Star

Complete

Every Day, I Miss You

The Empty Chair

Letting Go

Changed

All with You

Love Today and Forever

My Precious Love

Looking into Your Eyes

As One

You Are

Together, My Love

V.   The Truth I Know

My Passion

My Friends

The Sweetest Friend

Our Best Friends

Give Me Your Courage

Seeing Again

A Strong Family

The Long Road

The People

Soul and Spirit

The Heart of the Spirit

My Prayer

As I bow before You, Lord, in prayer,

I thank Thee for my life that You have spared.

For You are the rock in which my life's foundation lies,

No matter what anyone else sees, I want to be strong in Your eyes.

You are the light that guides my heavy feet...

In the walk of life, where no darkness, no sin, can defeat.

I pray, Lord, that You'll give the sick ones Your comfort and Your care,

I pray, Lord, that You'll be with Your saints everywhere.

I pray, Lord, that my neighbors will see Your love through me,

That we might both draw closer to Thee.

Lord, You are the one through which all blessings flow,

Bless me, Lord, wherever I may go.

Forgive my sins, Lord, for I am tempted each day,

Forgive those that have transgressed me, Lord, forgive them I pray.

But most of all, Lord, thank You for Your Son who died upon the tree,

He gave His life in humility - yes, for even me.

Be with me now, Lord, and carry me each day,

All of these things in Christ name I pray...Amen.

By Faith

By faith, I believe in Your majesty; by faith, I believe in Your love,

By faith, I will believe in Your word as I strive for Heaven above.

By faith, I pray I will walk Your pathway in times of happiness and strife,

For You are my strength, my hope, my guide; into Your hands, I put my life.

By faith, I will trust in Your love and Your wisdom to guide my way each day,

Although others may tear down my spirit, I will still press on the upward way.

Guard my soul each day, Lord, for Satan is crafty and often waiting to tempt me,

Help me each day to walk in Your light and be the example I am supposed to be.

By faith, my Lord, I will live my life each day by Your powerful, eternal plan,

By faith, I will have the courage to put my being, my life into Your hands.

Beautiful Day

I walk outside and see God's beautiful creation,

For I know He is with me, there is no hesitation.

I feel the warmth of the sun in the clear sky of blue,

For with The Lord, there is nothing I cannot do.

He is the commanding presence that is always in my life…

His presence is there in times of joy, happiness, pain, and strife.

That one day in Heaven is the greatest one day that will be,

My spirit will live with Him and be at peace for all eternity.

The sun and moon will pass, and time we'll no longer keep,

Yes, for all of His blessings in eternity, I will reap.

For the Lord God, I pray, will always be with me,

This is one of His beautiful days that He lets me see.

A Light in my Path

I stand in awe of Your power and matchless grace,

Oh Lord give me the strength to endure this life's race.

Comfort me, Lord, and I pray I always keep You deep in my heart,

For without You, Lord, my life would truly fall apart.

As I walk the narrow road each day and follow Your word,

Help me to understand the greatest message that man has ever heard.

Please be with me, Lord, and be the light to my path,

Protect me Lord…for I do not want to endure sin's wrath.

Your glory shines brighter than the sun, moon, or stars above,

For You are the awesome God; You are eternal love.

My Spirit

The spirit of man is strength from God built by His love,

For when we obey Our Father, blessings will reign from above.

We must put our lives in God's hands and believe with our might,

For we must follow Christ and walk by faith, not by sight.

For God will carry us when we cannot walk on our darkest days,

He will hold our spirit in His hands while molding us as clay.

He gives our spirit the courage to fight the temptations of this life,

He gives our spirit the power to face adversity and strife.

Lord, take my spirit and guide me through all of my days,

Until one day my spirit will be with You...each day I pray.

Guiding Love

The love of God will guide you throughout each day,

God's love is with you each time you meditate and pray.

His love will carry you when you do not have the strength to stand,

He will lift you up and show you another way or new plan.

God's love is His hand stretching out to lead your soul,

His love speaks through His word and will truly make you whole.

I Love You, Lord

I love you, Lord, for Your love, patience, mercy and grace,

I love you, Lord, for one day You will take me from this place.

Lord, when You will call me to Heaven it will be my new home,

I'll be in Your kingdom, Lord, for with You, I am never alone.

I will walk with my Savior, who bore my sin and died for me,

And freely suffered and gave His life upon Calvary's tree.

I love you, Lord for being almighty, long-suffering, just and true,

May Your love be shown through me in everything I do.

Life Looking Forward

Life is sometimes an unusual thing,

We must depend on Him who gives life and to Him our hearts and prayers bring.

For the time we have together,

Let us share our love for each other beyond measure.

Sometimes life causes us to grieve,

But we must keep our eye on what we're trying to achieve:

Heaven, and to share our love with one another,

To be re-united with our sisters and our brothers.

As children of God, to Him we must cling,

And pray to Him for strength to be able to handle anything.

In good times or in bad, in joyous times or in sad,

We should cherish the time we have.

Together, until we meet in Heaven again,

We must celebrate each other, and to its joy bring gifts.

Until united in Heaven, where happy memories never drift,

We'll meet again and spend an eternal day.

After we hear Him say "Enter in my faithful servant."

This is my prayer for us all, I pray.

An Empty Soul Filled

An empty soul the Lord Jehovah God can fill,

He will take your hand and with love your heart seal.

Let Christ guide you throughout each day of your life,

Depend on Him in times of joy, happiness, and strife.

In every way, God will love you; He will do His part,

Believing in Christ who died for you is where to start.

In all aspects you must love, respect, and put God first,

For our lives are only a vapor while here on this earth.

By faith we are blessed by His love, mercy, and grace,

Honor and trust Him; long to see His glorious place...

In Heaven, where we will shout, "We won the victory!"

Yes, we will walk with our Savior for all eternity.

The Faith Within

Lord God, give me the faith from within my heart,

May it never settle, never quench, never from You part.

In times when I am weak, may I ever look to You,

When I am strong, may Your love be ever so true.

As I struggle with this life, take my hand and guide me,

I pray I'll have courage and strength to only follow Thee.

No matter how harsh the cold days of winter can be,

I know You will send the springtime again for me.

The faith within my heart will guide my soul and comfort me,

I pray You direct and guard my life until Heaven I see.

Looking Forward to Heaven

Lord, I love You, and I'm willing to give...

My life to You, so I might live...

In Heaven with You and eternity spend...

Forever, where happiness and love will never end.

Lord, Your glory will now be seen as it was to me told,

As I walk with my Savior on the street of gold.

And rest in that home beyond the sky — my home above,

Where everything, Lord, is filled with Your love.

A Rose in Bloom

A rose in bloom...is beautiful, if only for a while,

Each season God creates them...it makes the world smile.

He fills the earth and nourishes its beauty everywhere,

For His lovely flowers are perfect...nothing else can compare.

He sends the rain and sunshine for their growth and to live,

To witness their beauty is a comforting peace only He gives.

A rose in bloom...is beautiful if only for a while,

There's no comparison to which He makes the heart smile.

Praise

The Lord is my strength and He is the light,

In Him there shall never be darkness, no night.

He gives me courage and shows His love each day,

He guides my footsteps and molds my heart as clay.

Through Him I have confidence in the choices I make,

For Heaven is my goal; I want to be there, whatever it takes.

Almighty Jehovah God, You are the foundation for my soul,

You are the rock on which I build my life that makes me whole.

Trust in God, my friends, for in Him you are never alone,

Be faithful and He will reward you with an eternal home.

Striving for Christ

Every day I live I thank God I am alive,

He blesses me each day and for Him I must strive.

For my goal is heaven — I want nothing less,

Oh, to be with Christ, my Savior, the Redeemed, and the Blessed.

I want to spend eternity without the presence of sin,

What a wonderful day that will be… where peace never ends.

Each day for Christ, I forever want to live,

Then on that wonderful day, peace to me He will give.

The Light in Me

There's a light that shines deep in my soul,

It is the love of Christ; it makes my life whole.

I pray others will be able to truly see,

His love; I pray it shines through me.

It is through His light my path is clear,

For when I walk with Him, I have nothing to fear.

I pray my example is one others can see,

His light, Christ's light; His love living through me.

Looking and Dreaming of Heaven

Every day in Your presence, Lord, will be an endless bliss,

There is nothing, not one Heavenly song I want to miss.

I want to be in Heaven, where we will never grow old...

And together with Christ, I want to walk the street of gold.

There with Christ I want to live one eternal day,

For Lord, every day this is my humble prayer I want to pray.

The Valley of Trust

I am walking in the valley of trust, looking and humbly waiting for a sign,

For when I am at my lowest, the Lord will carry me through difficult times.

I fight and I struggle because my life is blurred and anything but clear,

But I must believe in Him, for His love will always cast out every fear.

I have to have a strong faith and put my life wholly in His mighty hands,

For I eagerly await His guidance and direction as He shows for me His plan.

I am restless with my thoughts, but I must faithfully cling to Thee,

And clear my mind of doubt; for with His mighty strength, I am free.

Carry me, Lord, through this valley, and put my every fear to rest,

For I know with You, Lord, I will always be truly blessed.

Lord, my heart trembles as I walk through the valley this day,

Be with me, Lord, and carry me in Your arms…this I humbly pray.

You Are The One

You are the one that I can turn to,

You are the one that will always pull me through.

You are the one that I can rely on,

You are the one that will call me home.

You are the one in which I believe,

You are the one who gives me inner peace.

You are the one in which I have confidence each day,

You are the one to which I kneel in humbleness when I pray.

You are the one in which all goals I can achieve,

You are the one whose glory is more beautiful that I can conceive.

You are the one in whom I carry the spirit's shield and sword,

You are the one in which life exists, the great God Jehovah, my Lord.

The Rock of my Life

Humbly, I Bow

I bow before You, Lord, thanking Thee for the wonderful blessings of this life,

You have blessed me beyond measure and have held my hand in time of strife.

Humbly, I ask, Lord, to keep my life in Your mighty and powerful hand,

Guard my soul Lord, and deliver me from evil as I follow Your salvation's plan.

Lord, I am nothing without Thee; for my life, my being is in under Your control,

Guide and direct my footsteps for You, mighty Jehovah, are the keeper of my soul.

I pray I'll live with You one eternal day, Lord, in that mansion on high,

Where only love, happiness, and joy will reign; no tear shall ever fall from my eye.

Give me peace, O Lord, so my spirit will be free; for in life's battle, must win,

Crown me, O Lord when my time has passed, and I may hear, "to Heaven enter in."

Burdens Are Lifted by His Mighty Hand

As I take a step back from my life and breathe a fresh new air,

I feel the burdens I was bearing release and forever disappear.

No longer do I feed the heartache and pain that once consumed me with strife,

For now peace is finally present; new journeys will form, only optimism for my life.

The many lessons I've learned will help me to press on and seek higher plains,

For my faith has been held high by my Lord through the sunshine and the rain.

Though many challenges and difficulties arose to which I did not think I could stand,

My Father held my life and protected me with the power of His mighty hand.

My heart will heal and the sting of this past time will quickly vanish away,

For the future is bright…may His blessings continue to shine on my life each day.

I pray His peace may abound in my life and in those who I cherish and love,

I will continue to walk by faith and seek His guidance in my journey to Heaven above.

Held Through Each Journey

Lord, You have been with me throughout each journey of my life,

You have held me in the palm of Your hand in times of joy and strife

Where others have failed to see the hurt, anguish, and pain in my eye

You have carried me in Your arms and saw every tear I have cried.

I pray each day my faith will continue to hold strong in Your sight,

For I am greatly blessed by Your strength, Your love, and Your might

As new journeys begin, I pray my life will be pleasing to You,

I have a hope of Heaven where Your glory dwells above the bright blue.

Peace

Peace is what I want in prayer every day,

With God, there is peace when I obey His way.

Peace is perfected through God when Heaven is my home,

If I look to God, He will grant me peace, wherever I may roam.

Peace is being able to relax my restless and weary mind,

Peace is being able to pray knowing God's heart is kind.

Peace is knowing the ones who love you truly care,

For their spirit is kind, gentle, and loving towards you anywhere.

Peace is their love through The Father comforting my soul,

Peace through God comforts my mind that truly makes me whole.

Peace is where I pray to my Father, for in Heaven I want to be,

Peace is trusting my Father in all things, knowing His love for me.

Peace, perfect peace, is God granting me forgiveness from my sin,

Peace, perfect peace, is one day hearing God say "my servant, enter in."

For Me

For me, Jesus died and gave His precious life in agony,

For me, Jesus suffered, bled, and died on Calvary's tree.

For me, Jesus came from Heaven to live and die as a man,

For me, from the beginning of time...that was The Father's plan.

For me, Jesus was and is the perfect sacrifice that cleanses my sin,

For me, through His blood I will live forever and eternity spend.

For me, He wore a crown of thorns, was nailed by His hands and fee

For me, He lived a perfect life, died once for all and sin He did defea

Blessed Through Faith

Through God's love and kindness, I am truly blessed,

I pray I live for Him by faith in all of this life's test.

From everlasting to everlasting, The Lord is there,

He blesses my life, guards my soul, and is with me everywhere.

No greater love for me was given, than His son's sacrifice,

I pray I remain faithful and always follow my Savior Christ.

I pray my faith will be my strength until life shall end,

For with Him, I want to enter those pearly gates and eternity spend.

Every Day Lord, I Am Thankful

Every day, Lord, I am thankful for Your strength, Your love,

You are the great God Jehovah who reigns in Heaven above.

I am thankful for Your presence that guides my life following Your plan,

For You have kept me in the palm of Your mighty and powerful hand.

I am thankful for Your mercy, Your justice, and Your matchless grace.

I pray my light will ever shine; no darkness shall ever take its place.

I am thankful I can be called a child of Thine own,

For each day, I am one step closer to calling Heaven my home.

I Will

The game of life is one I will win,

I will achieve; I will conquer; I will overcome sin.

I will not give up on my aspirations and goals,

I will not quit until I reach that land where we'll never grow old.

I will fight life's battles and shun evil to its face,

And humbly pray to have strength to finish life's race.

Failure is never an option; winning is my only thought,

For every obstacle and every challenge - success is all that's sought.

I'll climb mountains and crawl through valleys to win this game,

I will have no fear; and with my effort, I will have no shame.

I will be strong; I will achieve my goals before my life shall end,

Then I will receive a new life in Heaven, and there eternity spend.

The Lord Is My Strength

I want to make the most of each day I have to live,

I am sustained by My Father's love and the blessings He gives.

I want to live each day as if it were on this earth, my last...

And leave behind the grudges that troubled me in the past.

Through My Father's love I want to embrace the beauty in life,

The courage and wisdom He gives are my strength for putting away strife.

Though hardships occur and others will bring my spirits down...

I will look to and strive for Heaven where I may wear a glorious crown.

With trust, I praise His name and put my life wholly in His hands,

By faith, I will glorify His name, follow His word and seek His eternal plan.

Legions of Angels

Legions of angels positioned themselves so they could see,

But they could only watch as He hung on Calvary's tree.

Eager to fight, mighty in number, they wanted to destroy all,

But all alone, Jesus suffered, both the great and the small.

He gave his precious life so we might with Him be able to live,

He gave everything…what a wonderful and selfless gift he gives!

Seeing His agony, the angels were ready for His call,

But Jesus carried our sins and died once for all.

The River

One day I will stand next to my Lord by the River of Life,

I will be firmly planted without sin, pain, grief or strife.

His glory will forever shine bright; for there will be no night,

There will be no darkness, only His love will be Heavens' light.

By its waters, I will gather with saints that lived their lives for Christ,

And be with our Savior who gave His life for us and paid sin's price

I will be there in Heaven for one beautiful, glorious eternal day,

I will be there with my Lord and Savior…this I humbly pray.

*co-written by Joe Adams

My Own Faith

My faith is my own; it is mine, and its strength I will not hide,

For it is with my Lord in Heaven I truly want to abide.

This world and its cares try to take control of my life each day,

But I want to be strong, be brave, with a strong faith... I pray.

I believe my Savior Jesus Christ gave His life for my sins,

I believe and I trust in Him that one day I will hear "Enter in."

I know for all who believe and truly follow Christ – Heaven awaits,

I want to feel God's perfect peace when entering those pearly gates.

I know I will sin; but Christ's blood covers each and every stain,

For without Christ, my life would truly be empty and sadly in vain.

My faith is truly unique because it is mine and mine alone,

It is my choice to follow Christ and have my faith, my own.

Stronger, I Rise

O Lord give me strength and wisdom… I humbly pray,

Give me the courage, Lord, to stand firm in Thee each day.

I will put away the sorrows and free my heart of the pain,

Let go of the tears that poured like an unstoppable rain.

Fill my soul with Your love, and grant me internal peace,

Bless me greatly, O Lord, and may the blessings never cease.

Take me from the valley, and set me on a mountain high,

Through Your powerful strength my spirit will be free to fly.

For my inner strength comes from wholly trusting in Thee,

I pray others may see Your wonderful love living in me.

By faith, I put my life and my being in Your mighty hand,

I am stronger, and now I rise because I followed Your plan.

One Day, Lord

One day, Lord, I want to walk with You in Heaven bright,

Where Your glory shines, and there will never be night.

One day, Lord, where sin is no longer, and I can finally breathe,

And behold the beauty of Your kingdom and never have to leave.

One day, Lord, when I can hear You say "Enter in and well done,"

That one day, Lord, will be where peace has truly begun.

One day, Lord, where I will truly have eternal joy and rest,

That one day, Lord, where I will be with You, forever blessed.

Going Home

I'm going home to that land beyond the sky,

I'm going home to Heaven above, where souls never die.

One day, I'll be there singing praises to God in His chorus on high,

There will be praise, joy, happiness; no tear will fall from my eye.

I'll see the glory and witness the beauty of my Father's hand,

For His majesty was from the beginning…it is His eternal plan.

I'm going to my Heavenly home, where my soul will reside,

It's there where I will walk with My Savior close to my side.

I'll Be There

One day, I'll be there, living in Heaven above,

Where I'll walk with my Savior and know His eternal love.

There, I'll praise God and sing praises in word and song,

I'll gather with my family in Christ for which I have often longed.

I'll live in a mansion on high and walk the street of gold,

I'll live there for one eternal day where we will never grow old.

I'll be there, where there will be no sorrow, pain, and sin,

Only peace, joy, and love...where I'll hear my Father say "Enter in."

When I Get There

When I get there...there will be a wonderful smile on my face,

A smile so grand nothing will be able to erase.

When I get there...I will see loved ones that have passed before me,

And now together with them I will live eternally.

My earthly life may have been filled with joy and possibly many tears,

But there is no pain in Heaven...I am with the Lord...I am finally here.

I had one goal throughout my life - to live with God forever,

And now I'm here eternally...for my soul no sin can sever.

I will be missed by loved ones still running life's race,

But I'll see them again and together we'll enjoy this beautiful place.

When I get there...I will walk with Christ, my Savior, on the streets of gold,

And live in eternal peace with Him forever, where we'll never grow old.

When I get there...my life's journey will be forever complete,

For with the Lord's help, I have accomplished my life's feat.

That Day I Await

There's a day that awaits my spirit, and it shall be grand,

For I long to be with God, putting my soul in His mighty hands.

I await that eternal day, where sin will no longer reign,

Where there's eternal joy and there will be no more sorrow or pain.

I await the day when I will be with my family in Christ forever more,

And stand by the River of Life and sing praises with them on its shore.

I await to be in Heaven and live in my mansion above,

For eternity – I will be with my Savior in peace, joy, and love.

Waiting on Heaven

O Lord, I'm waiting on Heaven and from sin to be set free,

For I want to wear a robe and crown and Heaven finally see...

Because of the blood of Christ, I can look forward to Heaven above

To be with my Father God and my Savior Christ Jesus who are love

I must be patient, and know the Lord will bless me as I continue in
life's race,

For I must look to Him for guidance and with His word keep a stead
pace.

Each day, I continually pray my faith grows in the Lord above,

And my faith will remain strong in truth, spirit, and love.

I know my Father will give me the strength I need to endure each da

Until my time has come for Christ to take me with Him... this I pra

I'm waiting on that trumpet to sound as this body returns to the du

Where I will rise to meet Him in the air; for it's in His hands I put
trust.

Direct me, Lord, until that one eternal day where I can be with Yo

And grant me that home in Heaven, where my life will be made ne

The Light that Leads Me

Seek First

Seek first the kingdom, for the time is at hand,

Live your life for Christ…that is God's plan.

Seek first the righteousness and goodness of His love,

Be faithful to God and He will send blessings from above.

Seek first the day evil and sin will forever be taken away,

Be humble and follow Christ, and you'll walk the street of gold
someday.

Seek first the reunion with your brothers and sisters in Christ,

For evil will not be there…sin cannot entice.

Seek first the glory to sing praise forever around His throne,

Love and serve God with all your might, and He will call you His
own.

Be with Me, Lord

Lord be with me throughout the day,

This is the simplest prayer I know how to say.

I need Thee in every moment of my being,

For You are the all-knowing and the all-seeing.

Be with me, Lord, for You are so wonderful, mighty, and great,

Be with me, Lord, for You know me better than my own self, every trait.

Be with me, Lord, for there are dangers and temptations I cannot see,

Be with me, Lord…for I am nothing without Thee.

Humility

I want to be humble in my life, I want to be meek,

It is not the praise of others I want to seek.

I want to be pleasing to God in the life I live,

To enjoy His blessings that He so graciously gives.

Praises will come when you are standing on a mountain high,

But down in the valley, others will leave you there to cry.

God's love for you will always and forever be,

Even though at times the pain of life is all I see.

I want to be humble and let my Savior strengthen my life,

And follow Him, the One they call The Christ.

Be strong, be confident, live for Christ with all your might,

And He will be with you no matter what others might do.

The Walk Each Day

Each day I walk with You, Lord, I feel complete in my life,

It's only when I fall to sin my world turns and fills with strife.

Help me, Lord, each day to fully have faith in Your matchless love,

Guard my soul, Lord, as I focus on that eternal home, Heaven above.

Give me strength, O Lord, as I journey as a pilgrim to this land,

Guide my life and hold my life in the palm of Your powerful hand.

Each day give me the courage to rely on and trust in Your mighty
word,

Help me to tell others the story of Jesus – the greatest message ever
heard.

Lord, bless and keep me until that one day I can be eternally with
You,

Be with me, Lord, for Your love is complete and forever will be true.

Life's Path

I walk a straight and narrow path that will lead me to my home,

It's a path where I walk with my Savior; for I am never alone.

A path of challenges and choices that each day I must face,

And pray I overcome the obstacles before me and keep a steady pace

To keep moving on the narrow path holding my Savior's hand,

Letting Him guide my steps as we walk towards the Promised Land

Holding on tightly for this life can be filled with heartaches and tears

But with His love I am at peace; for His presence conquers all fears

I must trust in Him with my whole being and put my life in His hands.

For He is my Savior; He knows my life, my purpose in God's eternal plan.

I pray when my last breath is taken and my journey comes to an end

That I will forever be in the presence of my Lord…in Heaven eternal spend.

Holding onto Your Hand

Lord, I'm holding tightly onto Your hand,

That is my life's purpose: my only plan.

You have given Your Son to die once for all,

Even me…though sometimes I slip and fall.

You carry my burdens when I cannot stand,

And hold my life in Your mighty, powerful hand.

Even though the world may oppress with strife,

I will hold Your hand because with You I have life.

I'm in life's race, focusing on Christ's eternal plan,

For I know He will guide and direct by holding my hand.

No matter how frigid and cold the winter may be,

Holding Your hand…I know there's a springtime for me.

Life and Its Storms

When the storms of life fall,

I know He will help me through them all.

Storm clouds may gather all around my life,

And a mighty storm may bring much strife.

A mighty wind could blow my humble life around,

And cut through my spirit and not settle down.

A volcano may erupt and may leave my heart open,

But the Father's love fills my life, and I shall never be broken.

Although disasters may one day have their place,

God still comforts me by His saving grace.

When the cold, dark storms of life fall,

I know He will help me through them all.

Abide with Me, Lord

Abide with me, Lord, for every day I need Thee,

Be with me, Lord, for I am weak, but Thou art mighty.

Keep my faith strong, so I can make it through each day,

Give me wisdom and knowledge; forgive my sins, I pray.

Hold my life in the palm of Your mighty and powerful hand,

Guide my life as I keep pressing on and living Your plan.

Direct my life and Your will be done in all things,

I long for one eternal day where I will eternally sing.

I'm Praying, Lord

I'm praying, Lord; I'm praying fervently for my life,

Grant me peace in a world of disappointments and strife.

Give me strength to help others wherever there is a need,

Grant me courage in planting Your word, Thy wonderful seed.

Forgive others, Lord, who have transgressions against me,

Forgive my sins, Lord; for I want my soul to be pure and free.

Guide and direct my footsteps, Lord, in my daily walk with thee,

I pray I will be a shining light for others around me to see.

Take and keep my heart, O Lord, by filling it with Your love,

For each day I'm praying, Lord, for my home, in Heaven above.

Strength and Faith

Give me strength, Lord, when I am weak,

To fight the world, to say it is only You whom I seek.

Help me, Lord, when others try to tear down the walls of my heart,

Keep me strong when I look to You, and mend them back, every part.

Give me faith, Lord, to know You will keep my spirit mighty,

So others will see Christ in me, and my soul will stay strong.

Give me strength and faith, Lord, to endure the world each day,

Give me strength and faith is the prayer I pray.

Lord, Be with Me

Lord be with me at every moment of my life,

Help me to always remember Your Son's great sacrifice.

I pray I can in His example live,

And show Your love to others as You so graciously give.

Help me to understand on You I have to rely,

Your will be done in all things…never question "Why?"

Help me to stand up to the devil and his crafty deeds,

Help me to spread Your word and in others plant a seed…

Of faith; to help me keep on life's pace,

And with You Lord finish life's race.

In Your kingdom is where I want to live,

You are the reason there is love to give.

With you there is no darkness, only light,

You are the reason my future is bright.

Trials and Temptations

There are many days filled with struggles in this life,

We face them with uncertainty, temptation, and strife.

Through obstacles and trials, our weakness can become strong,

If we focus on God and serving Him, we will not be wrong.

In the midst of temptations, we must lift our thoughts above,

And clear our minds of anger and fear; fill them with love.

We must stay strong and see the reward, for Heaven awaits.

Keep the faith, live for God - whatever it may take.

Live righteously and keep the faith in Him, my dear friend,

And when life has passed we can hear those words "Enter in."

Strength to Choose

Lord, You have given me the freedom to make choices in my life.

You have blessed and kept me; You have carried me through strife.

By faith, I want to follow and please You in this life I am in,

For all the cares of this world pulls at my life with all of its sin.

I know I'll never be perfect, but want righteousness in Your sight,

For one day, I want to enter those pearly gates…into Heaven brigh

Choices I make can break my spirit; no sunshine, only rain,

But You carried me through the storms and all the pain.

As I make the choices that will define my life, and guide my heart,

I pray Your guidance, Your strength, and Your love will never part

Help me, Lord, to see the direction to follow and that I must take.

Help me to keep Your word and love in the decisions I make.

Bless, keep, and help me to be strong by Your everlasting love,

Be with me, Lord, and guide my life until I reach Heaven above.

Lift Me Up

Lord, lift me up and hold me close in Thy hand,

For You are my strength, Lord, help me to see Thy plan.

You are the rock of salvation, the keeper of my soul,

I pray I find Your peace for it will truly make me whole.

Guide my steps and help me to walk faithfully unto Thee,

Give me the wisdom through the darkness of life I may see...

Your light...and walk each day in the path of Your will,

Your will be done in all things — in the name of Christ...Amen.

Trusting the Lord

Lord, You are the one in whom I trust my life,

I pray for strength, Lord, both in times of peace and in strife.

A servant for You, Lord, is what I want my life to be,

Bowing before You, Lord, in faith and hope of one day Heaven I w
see.

To give You all of my being, Lord, is my life's goal,

To walk with You, Lord, and in Your hands entrust my soul.

Humbly, I pray I will always look to Your word and obey,

To free my soul of sin, and be with You, Lord – this is my prayer I
pray.

Strength and Peace

As I walk down a broken road, I have only You to guide me,

Each step I take, I look to You, Lord, by faith to help me see...

Your plan for me; whatever Lord my purpose in life may be,

I know You'll give me strength for my each and every need.

Help me to be the man of whom You will be proud,

A light in the world and to You a joyful sound.

Always I pray, Lord, my faith in You increase,

For in Your love, Lord, I know I will have peace.

Grant me mercy, Lord, for each day it's Your kingdom I seek,

For I want to be numbered with the saved, the humble, and the meek.

Give me the strength, Lord, to endure this life, I pray,

And may I be with You in Heaven one day in peace, I pray.

Watch Over Me, Lord

Lord, You have provided for me my every need,

Keep my life in Your mighty hand, Lord…this I plead.

There are obstacles and uncertainties I face each day,

By faith I will put my cares in Your hands…this I pray.

Often I am discouraged by wanting life to fit my time,

But it's Your perfect timing that gives life its reason and rhyme.

Lord, I pray I am pleasing to You and the man You would have m.
be,

I pray Your continued blessings and You'll open doors of opportuni
for me.

There are so many areas in life Lord, I want success,

But one thing I do know, Lord - if I follow You, I will be blessed

Though friends may forsake me and may even leave my side,

I know, Lord, You are always with me and for me will provide.

This world can be very cruel, and darkness may cover my sight,

But I'll always look to You, Lord; for you are my guide and my lig.

Without You, Lord, I am a wave that is tossed to and fro by the se

But with You, Lord, I am blessed, and my soul is guarded and fre

I pray for Your mercy, Your grace; I pray for Your strength in lov.

I pray one day You'll guide me through those pearly gates above.

Take Me Home, Lord

Lord, I pray my faith will forever be strong in Thee,

I pray others will see Christ's light shine in me.

Through Your love, Lord, I want You to hold and keep my soul,

Until Heaven I reach; in the land where we'll never grow old.

And when that day comes, Lord, that I breathe my last,

Take me home, Lord, as I put this life in my past.

The Heart's Emotions

Only One

Only one love has truly ever filled my heart,

And I knew I loved her from the start...

When I first spoke to her and listened to her voice,

I knew it was love, and she was forever my only choice.

For I fell deep into the love in her eyes,

And knew to be with her, anything I would sacrifice.

Only one love have I ever known,

But my heart remains hopeful to make her my own.

I pray one day I will be her one and only love,

And forever live happily until we both reach Heaven above.

A Blessing

A blessing from God is what you are to me,

A blessing by His love you can only be.

You have a smile that shines ever so bright,

And a heart so loving it warms the night.

In no other dream will your beauty ever compare,

For I want to take the blessings of your goodness with me everywhere.

The depth of your kindness is unmatched and knows no bounds,

Through God's love is where the strength of your soul is found.

For your presence is as beautiful as a dream.

A blessing from God is what you are to me,

A blessing by His love you can only be.

You're the Poem in My Heart

The name written on my heart belongs to you,

It is a name that is engraved and forever will be true.

Surrounding your name are words that express the love I feel,

Words of care, compassion, and faithfulness - those are genuine and real.

The words are arranged in a poem that is so beautiful, only you are worthy to read...

Of my love for you, how you meet my every care, every need.

I wrote the words with an arrow that I received from above,

For God sent the arrow to me out of His love.

Each day there is a new verse written by your loving grace,

For your poem will always be, it will never lose its place.

You are the poem that resides in my heart,

And will forever stay because it was yours from my life's start.

Amazing

An amazing person you are with a beautiful heart,

God gave and blessed you with that from your life's start.

For your eyes could even warm the coldest of days away,

And He gave you a smile that brightens each day.

He is the source from which your strength abides,

For He is ever with you - yes, always at your side.

Your care, warmth, and beauty came from His hand,

For the amazing person you are…it was in His plan.

Unconditional Love

I love you unconditionally with all of my heart,

I pray now our love never ceases; it never parts.

Without you, emptiness would reign in my soul,

With you, my heart is mended and whole.

For I am complete when I look into your eyes,

Perfection is with you, there is no compromise.

I will give my love to you, now and forever,

For, my love, you are my life's treasure.

Only Know to Say

I love you; that's all I know to say,

For you live in my heart each and every day.

Words cannot describe how your love makes me feel,

My love to you, forever, will remain real.

I am yours from this point in my life,

I want you to forever be my loving wife.

The Lord has given me a beautiful choice,

For we only seek His wisdom and His voice.

I love you; that's all I know to say,

For you live in my heart each and every day.

Always and Forever

I want to be yours, always and forever,

I will never leave your side, no never.

In my thoughts, I can hear your sweet voice,

You are mine and I am yours; that is our choice.

Only sweet words from me you will hear,

And I'll be there to wipe away every tear.

I will never live another day without you in my heart,

For your spirit has been there from my life's start.

Always and forever will my love for you only be,

You have given my life a beauty only I can see.

The Bright Star

There's a bright star shining in my life tonight,

Her glow brightens even the darkest part of night.

For her beauty and her grace is not known to all,

But her sweet voice echoes each time she calls.

The Lord is her strength and in Him she has faith,

Faith that does not waiver, for she has God's grace.

She testifies to others by courage because of His love,

And prays for them to have strength in Heaven above.

There's a bright star shining in my life tonight,

Her glow brightens even the darkest part of night.

Complete

As we start our life's journey together,

Our love for each other shall never fade, no never.

I see your smile and my fears melt away,

I only want to have that feeling each day.

I look deeply in your eyes and I see a man - yes, that is me,

A man that you make me want to be.

Until at Heaven's gates the Lord we greet,

You are the only one that makes me complete.

Every Day, I Miss You

I miss you; every day I live, I miss you,

I'm waiting on my heart to be rescued.

Rescued from the everyday fear...

A fear that over you, I'll shed more tears.

I cannot go on feeling this way,

I feel your presence is near every day.

I have a hope I clearly seek...

A hope once again our lives will meet.

And meet together heart to heart,

Our hearts from one another will never again part.

I miss you; every day I live, I miss you,

I'm waiting on my heart to be rescued.

The Empty Chair

I look at the empty chair sitting beside me,

I feel the emptiness... so clear I can see.

This is not how I wanted my life to be,

Others tell me to be thankful I am free.

I've let go and truly put that life in the past,

And now I'm looking for a beautiful love that will last.

My heart yearns for a strong love filled with care,

I'll take it forever with me...any and everywhere.

What I want is for my life to be filled with peace,

A beautiful, faithful, loving wife, whose love will never cease.

Where her kindness can truly never be measured,

Her love will be my joy, my happiness, my treasure.

I have so much love I truly want to give,

To have a love so true, faithful and forever live.

I want her to walk with me in life in every stride,

With her hand in mine...forever close to my side.

Letting Go

Lord, I will look to You and let go of my past,

Into Your hands, my cares and concerns I will cast.

I've let go of the reins where she held my heart,

And said goodbye as she destroyed every part.

As I look forward now from this new day,

I will put my life in Your hands…this I pray.

I will let go of cares in life I cannot control,

And know You'll watch over me and guard my soul.

By faith, I know I will be able to see,

What You, my Lord, have in store for me.

Giving my heart to one who will hold it strong,

And find her, the one…to whom it belongs…

There is one day I'll be able again to say,

"I love you, my love and my best friend."

She'll be the right one; this I will know,

To her my heart belongs…never letting go.

Changed

Since the first time I saw your smile, my life has changed,

And now I only think of love when I hear your name.

For the first time, I understand what love truly means,

For because of you, my life has become a beautiful dream.

I pray each day my love will be a strength to you,

For your Love is my light, and in love I will forever be true.

Your love and kindness has changed my life in a beautiful way,

For the warmth of your love is what I carry in my heart each day.

With the love of your heart and your hand in mine, I am forever complete,

By the strength of our love, there is nothing we cannot together defeat.

All with You

All that I am and all that my being could ever be,

Is because of your love; that, I want you to see.

The warmth of your heart filled my life with love,

You are my dream sent from the Lord God above.

I'm strengthened and comforted by your kind words,

Within my heart, my soul, your voice will forever be heard.

Each day I see your beautiful smile comforting my heart,

You are the joy in my life that blesses each day as it starts.

I thank the Lord above that your love makes my life whole,

You are my angel; you are the love that comforts my soul.

Love Today and Forever

Let me hold you, my love, in my arms today,

And I will never let go; my love is here to stay.

You are the smile I will have for the rest of my life,

Holding my hand, side by side, my beautiful wife.

You are the sparkle that shines in the stars above,

You are the rose that blooms in my heart, my love.

You are my sunshine when the day is filled with rain,

Without you, the words of my heart would be written in vain.

Today, my love, I pledge all of my love to you,

And until I breathe my last, I will forever be true.

My Precious Love

Though I have not always known who you would be,
My dream of you was easy to see...
My precious love.

Now for some time we have been together,
I know I cannot live my life without you, no never...
My precious love.

As I journey through this life,
I can only make it with you as my wife...
My precious love.

Now the only thing is for our love to seal,
Because our love for each other is so real...
My precious love.

Looking into Your Eyes

When I look deep into your eyes, this is what I see,

Your love shining through the man that I want to be.

I see your warmth, your kindness, your love so strong,

For with you, in this moment, is right where I belong.

You are the rose that blooms and never fades away,

For it has grown in my heart, and I will cherish it every day.

I know your beautiful love will forever remain true,

Place your hand in mine; I will remain ever faithful to you.

As One

On this day we begin our life's journey as being one,

We'll walk hand in hand together, following God's Son.

From this very moment in time, we'll no longer be apart,

But we will be equally united together, forever as one heart.

We leave behind the memories and thoughts that filled our past,

For our love will each day grow stronger and will forever last.

O God, our God, direct our footsteps and guide our way,

Until at last Heaven we reach…this is our prayer we pray.

You Are

You are the one to which I give my heart,

From your love, I hope, I never will part.

When the dark clouds surround my life,

You are my sunshine, my beautiful wife.

You give your all and your love comforts me,

Because of you, I can be the man I am meant to be.

You are the spark that ignites my fire,

You and only you are my one true desire.

You are the voice of reason I hear each day,

I do not want to spend a day without you in any way.

You are the beauty that makes my day bright,

You are the star that guides me in the night.

Turn the pages of my heart, and you'll find love to read,

I pray each day I can give you your every need.

I pray each day you will see,

What your love does to me.

If nothing else in this world is true,

Remember my love, I love you.

Together, My Love

I love you, I love you, with all of my heart,

The first time we said it to each other was our life's start.

You are my best friend, my love and my all,

We'll walk the mountains of life both great and small.

Together, we'll take on the challenges of this life,

With your hand in mine, forever being my beautiful wife.

Together, my love we'll press forward and look to our future bright

Follow my lead, my darling angel, as we strive for Heavens' light.

If I only know one thing in this world to be true,

Is that every day I will pledge my love to you.

Promise me this, each day you will say,

I love you for the rest of my days.

*written for April

The Truth I Know

M

y Passion

My passion is one I no longer want to hide,

It is a zeal within my heart I want the Lord to guide.

I pray my words will describe the love within my heart,

And encourage those who are searching for a fresh start.

I am very thankful I can explain the creativity my mind brings,

Through God's will, I explain the thoughts of my soul as it sings.

My passion is a voice I am now showing to the world,

It's a love that burns deep within; it comforts my soul.

My Friends

My brothers are who I call my closest friends,

They stand behind me and will abide with me unto any end.

My friends are those who patiently listen to me speak...

And will help me to remain humble and meek.

They are with me to share a laugh and even a tear,

For they are always with me throughout my years.

I am very blessed to have true friends of this worth,

For they are valued more than any treasure on this earth.

I am proud and honored to call my brothers, my closest friends,

For they will be in my heart unto my life's end.

*written for my brothers

The Sweetest Friend

The sweetest friend - what words can describe a beautiful heart?

God's love is her strength that with her will never part.

She is a wonderful blessing... worthy of honor,

For her life has a beautiful light which glows around her.

Her kindness is unmatched and compassion knows no bounds,

She is selfless and strong, all joy surrounds.

My sweetest friend will forever reign close to my heart;

Our friendship is a blessing from above... it shall never part.

*written for Shanna

Our Best Friends

Our best friends…they have a tail, four legs and paws,

They love us unconditionally without any cause.

They sit, they shake, and they love to have their belly rubbed,

For every day we show them how much they are loved.

Their smile is infectious and so very sweet -

Though they might bite us when they do not get a treat.

If your best friend is a large dog or even a little cat,

They'll always love you…remember that.

Give Me Your Courage

Lord, grant me the courage to face the trials of life throughout the day,

Give me the wisdom to understand the obstacles that are in my way

Give me strength as I put my humble life in Your mighty, powerful hand,

Guard my soul and give it the direction it needs as I trust and follow Your plan.

I will face trials, heartaches, and many unforeseen hurdles in my life

May I be humble before You, and find Your courage as I take on strife.

May You lift me up and give my weary heart Your inner, loving peace

Lord, give me the courage I need, and may Your love never cease.

Seeing Again

Although a loved one has passed, their memory will always reign in our hearts,

It's a beautiful memory; it shall never leave us, no it shall never part.

We long for one day to be in Heaven where we will see them again,

Where we will be with our Father God and Christ, our brother and friend.

We miss our loved ones each day, but know they are in a better place,

We want to be together with the Lord where we are saved by His grace.

For now we must press on; we must keep our hearts and minds clear.

We must follow Christ; let Him fill our lives with happiness and cheer.

Lord, I pray our loved ones are with you in Your arms today,

Lord, I pray Your will be done in each and every way.

A Strong Family

A strong family can be described as the love of cherished relatives and friends,

They are the people who will care deeply for us until our lives shall end.

The strength of a strong family is built on love for the Father above

He is the foundation in which our lives are based through His wonderful love.

Each day we carry our families' love, honor, and courage within the depths of our hearts,

For no matter how discouraging times can be, their love, care, and strength will never part.

A strong family will stand by us, stand behind us, and comfort us in times of grief and strife,

They are our strength spiritually, emotionally, physically...worth more than any treasure in life.

A strong family will give every ounce of their beings to see a smile upon our faces,

A strong family will help guide each other to Heaven...helping to win life's race.

A strong family encourages each other to show love and be a great example for others to see,

An example of strength, humility, and respect through love...for that is what has been shown to me.

By faith, a strong family will look to the Father for wisdom and guidance through His love,

And follow His direction with understanding of our hope eternally of Heaven above.

The Long Road of Life

On the long road of life, our troubles can cause us to trip and fall,

There are hardships which bring us down...as we try to walk tall.

There are many dangers in this life we will face.

With only one belief: that patience and courage can keep pace.

And we must face life with all of its many concerns,

For we are responsible; we decide the best way in which to turn.

We have examples of those that have walked before,

But only courage can give us the power to walk a little more.

We have to keep moving and never stand still or sit,

We must press on with diligence and never, never, quit...

We can walk the road and press on another day...

Walking the road of life; handling the obstacles in our way.

The People

The people I love, I carry with me every day,

May the Lord bless them; this is my prayer I pray.

Sometimes, I can only hear their voice,

Sometimes thinking of them is my only choice.

Every day, I will carry them in my heart,

I carry them there so we'll never be apart.

Whether friends or family, makes no difference to me,

For we are all apart of God's eternal family.

The people I love know my struggles, my every fear,

The people I love are my happiness, they bring much cheer.

Each person brings a unique aspect that has a special part,

They will always be with me, for I carry them in my heart.

Soul and Spirit

My soul and spirit are expressed and written on my heart,

Holding on to His hand and praying His strength will never part.

Every day, I have looked to Thee for guidance and direction in my life,

I know there will be obstacles and trials that will bring me strife.

It is by His strength I will hold tightly to His mighty, powerful hand,

Through His love and His guidance, I will overcome, if that is His plan.

My soul seeks His wisdom for strength as I live this life each day,

My spirit seeks His peace to one day in Heaven be carried away.

Lord, I pray my heart will be full of Your love as I look to Thee,

Hold my life in Your hands, Lord, and guard my life until Heaven I see.

Closing The Door

I want to say thank you to everyone who helped with accomplishing this work, this goal in my life. Writing is a passion, it is an expression, and it has been and is a way I deal with life. I have a pen and a blank piece of paper...I can express my heart, soul, and spirit in written form. Being able to express my love, praise, and thankfulness to the Lord has helped me through life. One of the greatest aspects of writing poetry for me is helping others. I know that poetry is not for everyone, but if my words can help in others' lives, it is worth writing every word. If I can write something that brings someone closer to God, to their family and friends or just to be a positive influence...I truly cannot put into words how much that means to me. God has blessed me with creativity and to be able to express my thoughts and feelings in written form. I am very thankful I can help others see His love, greatness, might, strength, and peace.

Poetry, to me, is the crossroads of creativity and emotion. It is sharing and expressing my heart. But then again, I think it is simple. When I was younger, I did not understand fully when someone said they were passionate about their work or some cause they pursued. I only understood in the sense of being passionate about playing and watching sports, but nothing more. I discovered being passionate through the process of writing "_Brothers Always_." It changed my life. It taught me hard work, having a goal, and not stopping until I reached it. That will forever resonate throughout my life. I may write more poems or stories, but nothing I could write will ever equal what "_Brothers Always_" taught me about myself and about life.

When I say this is a personal work that is an understatement. I've always looked at stories and poetry differently. Stories, I can create a character that hides and develops emotions within themselves throughout the story. Poetry, is straightforward. There's no hiding emotions. Who you are and what you think truly are seen. I did not know if I would ever write or publish another book after "_A Look Inside_," but the idea and the motivation to publish (if only this one last book) was one of the positive things I could see. There's no other title I could give this book besides "_Soul and Spirit._" It's the words of my heart that reside in this book. I cannot express it in any better way. I knew if I was able to publish this work, I was not going to hold anything back. I was going to leave everything on the field, because I did not know if I would ever see the field again. I am doing this for me.

It may seem strange or different to have so many forwards. Each person has been a strong influence in my life. They have been with me in joyous days and dark. In both instances, they have remained strong for me and have been the encouragement I needed. Through God's love, they have been a rock in my life. This is my way of saying "thank you" to them. I would not be the person I am today without them. "_Soul and Spirit_ "is closing the door on the writing and emotions brought from a difficult chapter in my life. It is the way I have expressed my deepest emotions and poured out my heart in written form. For so many years in my life, especially the younger years, I did not want to show this side of myself. This side only came out with very few, and I look back and I wish I had let more see. With anything I do in life, I want to put my heart in those pursuits. That is how I have had success - putting my heart wholly into what am doing. I do not believe, for me, there is any other way. Yes, sometimes that hurts because I do not always see the negative side of life. But who I am and what I've become has been led by my heart. That is where "_Soul and Spirit_" has developed; because I have put my heart, soul, and spirit into this work. I do not know any other way

It has been a journey for me and now with its release the door on those emotions that drove this work for me can close.

There have been so many family and friends that have been there for me emotionally and spiritually. I want to say thank you. The poem "A Strong Family" was written because of all the love and support I have been shown. It is one of my favorite poems I have ever written. My family is not just relatives. It is friends, spiritual family – it is my loved ones. When I was at the lowest point of my life, they stepped up, and through God's love, carried me. One thing I have found is everyone, no matter who you are, needs help at some point. We should help each other. I strongly believe that is the way the Lord intended it – for us to help each other and be there for each other. We cannot always handle life on our own; many times we need others to be strong for us. I see how the Lord has put others in my life for strength, for encouragement…this is definitely an inspiration in my writing. I want Him to be glorified through my writing for who He is, for leading me, loving me, guiding me, and knowing what I need. He is the Almighty God.

The only possible way I overcame many obstacles was by putting my life in God's hands and praying His strength would keep me. I can look back now and see how God always took care of me. I see how He turned tragic situations into good. Romans 8:28 reigns true in my life. I see how through His love I became stronger.

Made in the USA
Middletown, DE
23 November 2018